EXPLORING ARTIFICIAL INTELLIGENCE

# HOW AI WORKS

Lisa Idzikowski

Lerner Publications ◆ Minneapolis

**For my family**



Lerner Publications Company
An imprint of Lerner Publishing Group, Inc.
241 First Avenue North
Minneapolis, MN 55401 USA

For reading levels and more information, look up this title at www.lernerbooks.com.

Main body text set in Aptifer Sans LT Pro.
Typeface provided by Linotype AG.

**Editor:** Nicole Berglund **Designer:** Viet Chu **Photo Editor:** Nicole Berglund

**Library of Congress Cataloging-in-Publication Data**

Names: Idzikowski, Lisa, author.
Title: How AI works / Lisa Idzikowski.
Description: Minneapolis : Lerner Publications , [2025] | Series: Exploring Artificial Intelligence | Minneapolis : Lerner Publications, 2024. | Includes bibliographical references and index. | Audience: Ages 8–12 | Audience: Grades 4–6 | Summary: "AI is everywhere, from robot soccer games to the smartphones in our pockets. Readers will learn the history of this technology, how it works, and how it continues to improve"— Provided by publisher.
Identifiers: LCCN 2024012985 (print) | LCCN 2024012986 (ebook) | ISBN 9798765647912 (lib. bdg.) | ISBN 9798765661680 (pbk.) | ISBN 9798765654477 (epub)
Subjects: LCSH: Robotics—Competitions—Juvenile literature. | Robots—Juvenile literature.
Classification: LCC TJ211.2 .I39 2025 (print) | LCC TJ211.2 (ebook) | DDC 006.3—dc23/eng/20240509

LC record available at https://lccn.loc.gov/2024012985
LC ebook record available at https://lccn.loc.gov/2024012986

Manufactured in the United States of America
2-1013194-53352-8/29/2025

# TABLE OF CONTENTS

## INTRODUCTION

# LOOK AT THAT!

Two soccer players squared off on the field before jumping into action. They tackled and blocked each other. The players tripped, fell, and got up. Then they ran down the field and scored a goal. It sounded like an everyday one-on-one game. But these soccer players were not at practice or playing casually during recess. These players were robots. Artificial intelligence (AI) guided every tackle, block, fall, and goal.

In 2023 these AI-fitted soccer robots appeared all over social media and TV. Some viewers might have been shocked at the sight. Others cheered on each robot's goal or tackle. Computer experts at DeepMind, a Google research lab, celebrated. Their AI-powered bots had taught themselves how to play.

The company DeepMind was created in 2010. Google purchased it in 2014.

Scientists and engineers at DeepMind have a goal. They want to create AI that can reason and learn without help from people. Computers and robots usually run on software programmed by people. But not these special soccer-playing bots. They run on AI trained by engineers at DeepMind. It took about two weeks for the AI to learn how to move like a human soccer player. Then it was put into a robot. The knee-high robot jumped into action.

An engineer assembles a robot.

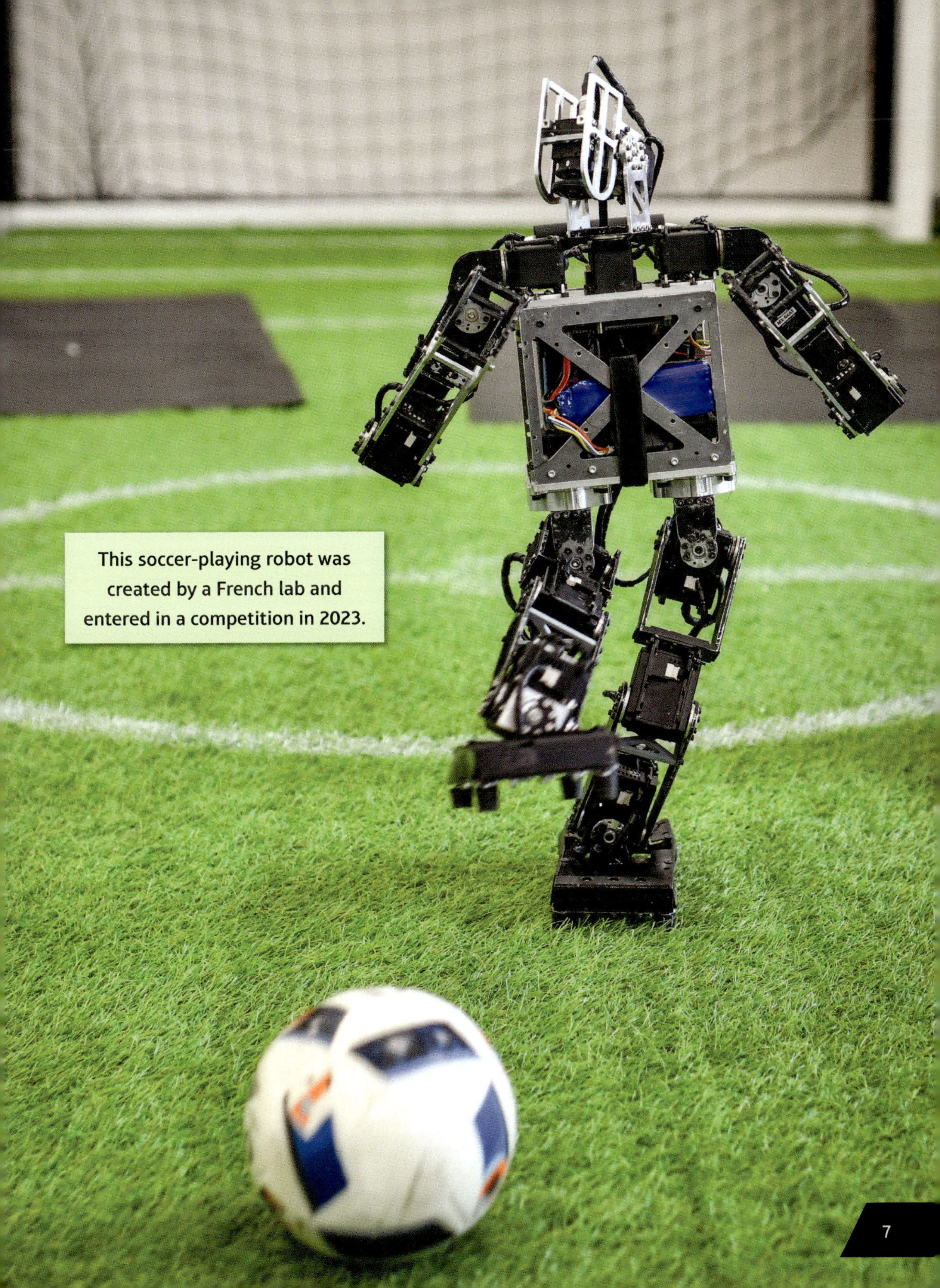

This soccer-playing robot was created by a French lab and entered in a competition in 2023.

Thomas Edison with the light bulb he invented in 1879. Edison had to overcome many hurdles in the development of his invention, just as AI developers have with theirs.

## CHAPTER 1

# COMPUTERS THAT LEARN

For thousands of years humans have found ways to make life better. They learned to use fire. They found shelter and made tools for hunting. Then people grew their own food. Over generations people discovered new technologies. They harnessed electricity and perfected light bulbs. The world kept changing. People faced bigger and bigger challenges. Jobs, work, and technology advanced along the way.

Engineers and scientists wanted to solve problems more quickly and easily. People invented a new technology: computing machines. In the 1940s the Electronic Numerical Integrator and Computer (ENIAC) could add five thousand numbers in one second. The press called it a giant brain. People wondered about these machines. Could they think like a person? Some experts thought so.

Workers operate the ENIAC by moving cables and switches.

In the summer of 1956, a group of researchers met at Dartmouth College in New Hampshire. From June to August, they worked on special projects. Their efforts defined a new area of science. They called it AI. The researchers believed they could make machines as intelligent as people. Then only a handful of computers existed. At first, computers were not very fast or powerful. This did not stop the scientists.

Dartmouth College opened in 1769, and it has become a top school in the United States.

## Programs and Robots

Computer engineers and scientists tried new things to advance computers. They experimented with computer programs and robots, such as Shakey, that used AI. They wanted to make intelligent machines and computer programs that could act like people. What a huge challenge!

Engineers build a robot.

Expert systems were created as AI improved. Programmers coded the medical knowledge of experts, such as doctors, into programs. This helped advance the medical field. Mycin was one of the first expert systems invented for the medical field. It used a patient's symptoms to help doctors figure out a treatment. It helped doctors treat blood infections.

Mycin was created in 1972 at Stanford University in California.

## Machine Learning

Imagine a day without social media or video games. How about streaming movies and playing music? Machine learning makes all these possible. It is a way to use AI.

Machine learning was invented in the 1950s. Computers that used it were different from those that used other types of AI. Computers learned without being programmed to do so. Think of cooking. Recipes have exact directions to make something. With machine learning algorithms, a computer learns to program itself through experience or recognizing patterns, not with a recipe.

Recipes teach us to make new foods, and experienced cooks can make food without recipes.

Machine learning algorithms learn from data.

## Teaching Itself

Machine learning algorithms teach themselves using data. They need lots of it. Data can be photos, words, numbers, and even pictures of pets. Supervised machine learning is the most common algorithm. For example, an algorithm could be trained by viewing pictures of cats. The pictures would be labeled with the word *cat*. After seeing so many pictures, the machine would be able to recognize a cat on its own.

# It's Shakey, the World's First Smart Robot

In the late 1960s, Shakey, one of the first AI-controlled robots, powered up. Standing 5 feet (1.5 m) tall, the world's first smart robot understood about one hundred words. It was housed at Stanford University in California and used wheels to roll from room to room. Shakey saw the world through a TV camera and felt things through catlike whiskers. Shakey's software and algorithm, A*, is still used in computer games.

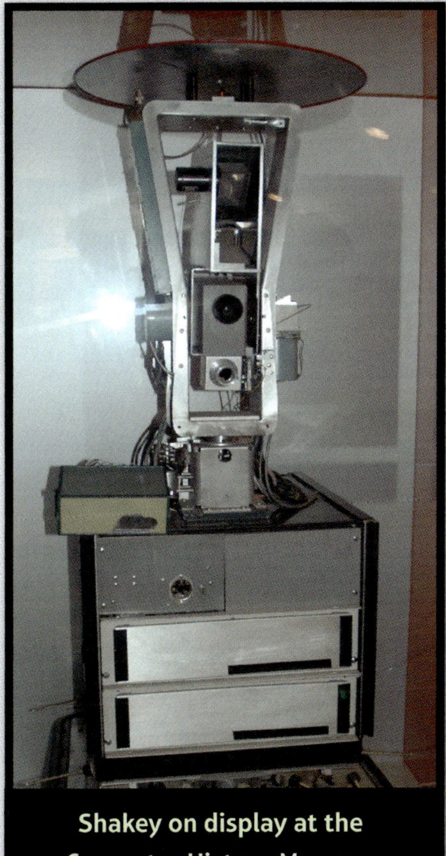

Shakey on display at the Computer History Museum in California

In unsupervised machine learning, the system sorts through data and looks for patterns. During reinforcement machine learning, the machine learns by trial and error. DeepMind's soccer robots learned how to play using this type of AI.

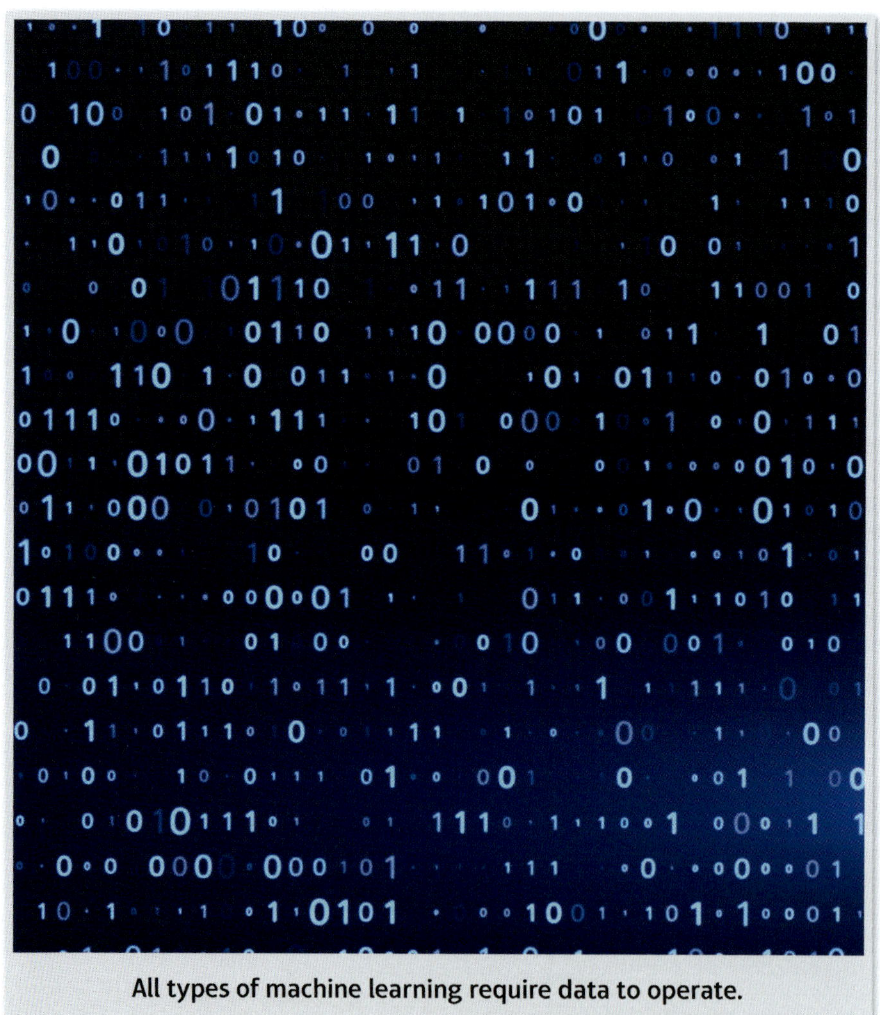

All types of machine learning require data to operate.

Tesla's Model S electric car, released in 2021, uses AI when self-driving.

## CHAPTER 2
# DEEP LEARNING

Imagine a self-driving car heading down a road. A school is up ahead, and lots of people are walking around. Nearby, two kids step off the sidewalk. The car sees them and immediately stops. Later that day, it's time to shop. You can jump online and search for a pair of jeans. It's easy to find your perfect size.

In each of these examples, deep learning is hard at work. Deep learning is the way a machine learns through experience. It operates self-driving cars. It also powers Amazon's algorithm to help people find what they are looking for.

The company Amazon was created in 1995 as an online bookseller, though it grew in the following decades and now sells almost anything.

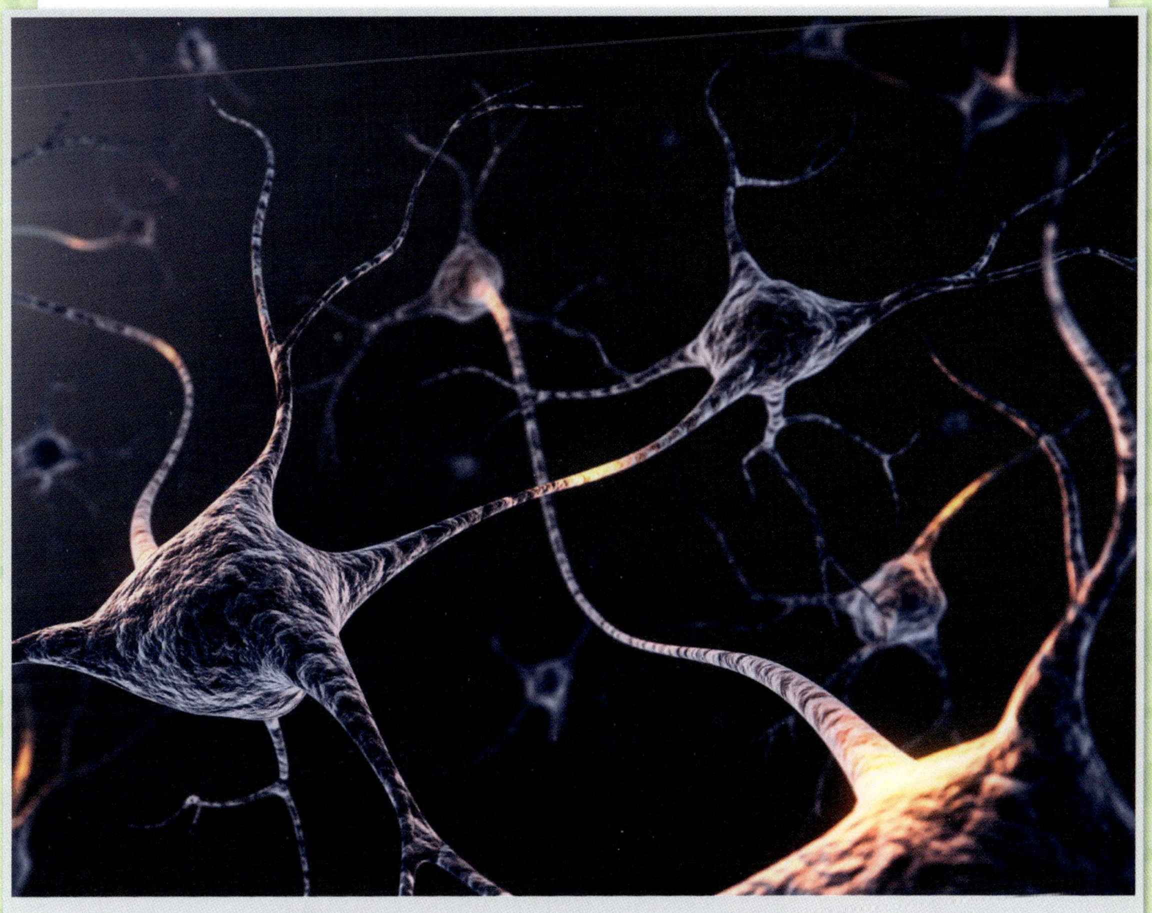

An illustration of the neural network in a human brain

## AI, Machine Learning, or Deep Learning?

AI is a computer science technology. Machine learning is a subset of AI. Deep learning is a subset of machine learning. Machine learning and deep learning both use a special algorithm called a neural network. Deep learning networks are larger. They have more than three layers.

## Like a Brain

The human brain is powerful. It controls everything that a person feels, thinks, sees, and does. All this is made possible by the brain's microscopic cells called neurons. A person's brain has about one hundred billion of them. Each neuron is connected to thousands of others. Activity in this network of neurons makes the brain work.

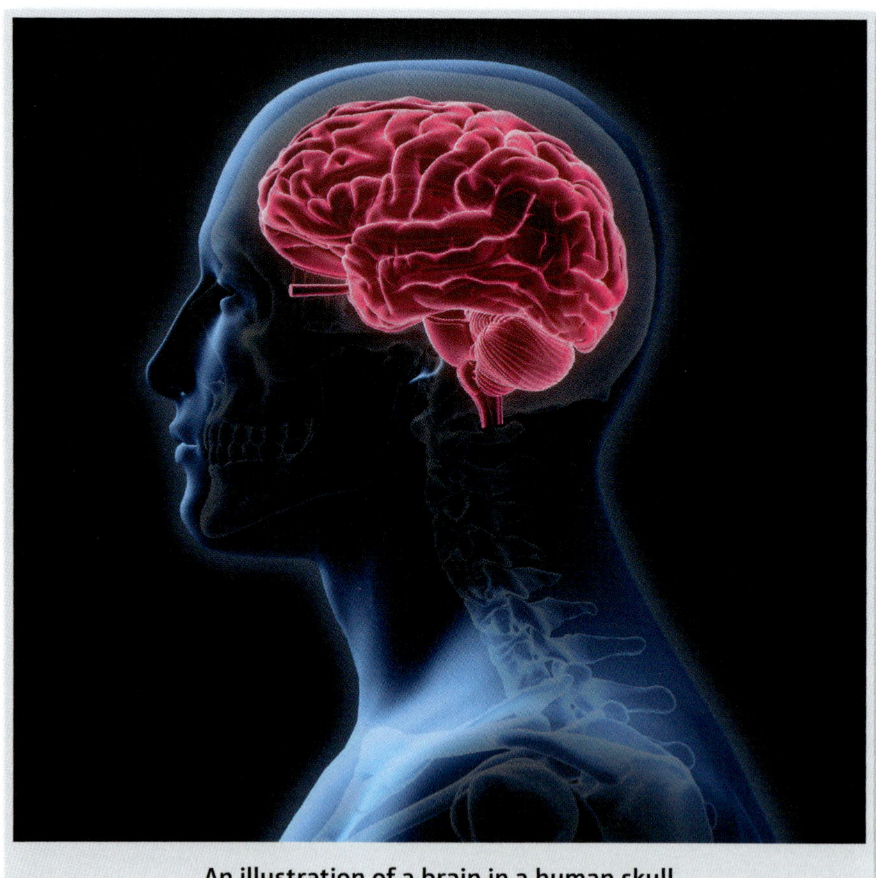

An illustration of a brain in a human skull

# GEOFFREY HINTON

Computer scientist Geoffrey Hinton is called the godfather of AI. During his career, he modeled AI systems on the human brain. His work on neural networks has made advanced machine learning possible. Hinton has earned many awards. In 2018 he received the Turing Award. In 2023 he was named to *Time* magazine's list of the 100 most influential people in AI.

Geoffrey Hinton speaks at an event in 2023.

Some computer systems are modeled after the human brain. They are made of artificial neurons that become an artificial neural network. These networks can be trained. Information is fed into a machine's network. Layers of neurons handle the information. Results flow out. Feedback gives the machine information. The system learns from the experience. This is what deep learning is. Self-driving cars learn to drive through practice. Online shopping algorithms learn to suggest new products from how you shop.

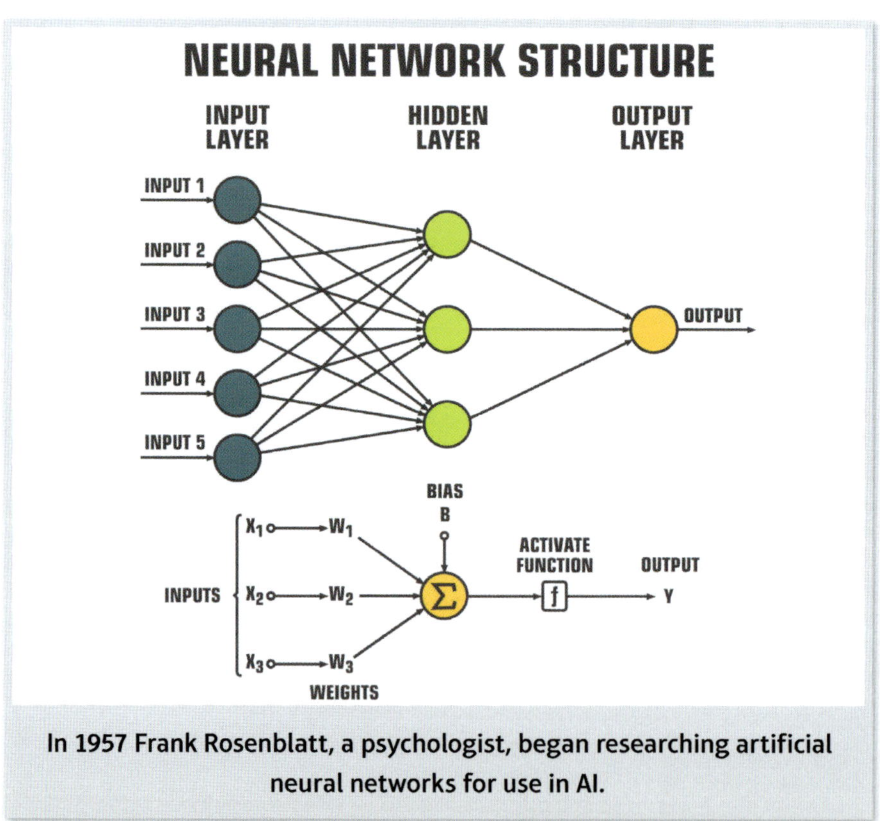


In 1957 Frank Rosenblatt, a psychologist, began researching artificial neural networks for use in AI.

# Deep Learning Helps Save Whales

Six of the thirteen great whale species are endangered. Many people around the world work to protect these giant mammals. How do scientists learn where whales are or how they travel in the oceans? They listen to and record whale songs and sounds. This underwater data is then handled by AI. The TensorFlow deep learning system takes over. This AI identifies different whale sounds and helps scientists with whale conservation efforts.

The North Atlantic right whale is one of the most endangered whale species.

CHAPTER 3

# LET'S CHAT

People on the go often turn to AI technology. Students needing help with homework might ask, *Siri, what's seven times eight*? Others might want to know which coat to wear. *Hey, Alexa, what's the temperature today*? Hungry people want somewhere to eat. *Hey, Google, are there any pizza places nearby*? Virtual assistant technology helps people every day.

## Talking but Not Understanding

About sixty years ago, the first chatbot appeared. Eliza, a software program, acted like a therapist. People chatted with Eliza by typing on a keyboard. A computer showed Eliza's answers on-screen.

Did the program understand people? No. The system used its program to find a reply.

Chatbots are computer programs that communicate with people. Early programs had built-in rules. If a person asked a certain question or said a certain word, the machine gave a programmed answer.

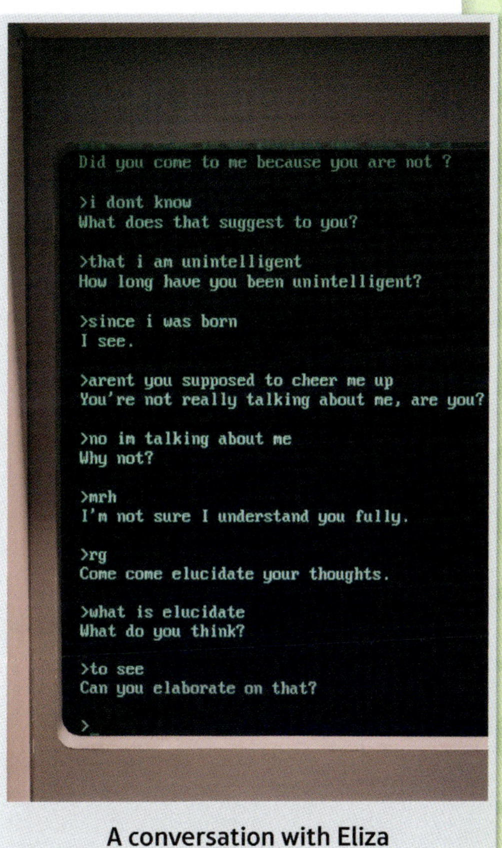


A conversation with Eliza

## Chatbots Got Smarter

Technology improved, and so did chatbots. Conversational AI made chatbots seem smarter. Users could talk to these virtual assistants. Machine learning, data, and natural language processing made it happen. This technology is advanced. It allows machines to use and understand human speech. The machine can then talk with people.

Virtual assistants understand voice commands.

## Smarter Yet

Do some machine systems seem even smarter? It's easy to think so. Generative AI models trained on deep learning create things. They can write stories or answer questions. They carry on conversations. They even create videos or pictures. They do this by taking data from the internet and combining it in different ways.

ChatGPT and Gemini are examples of generative AI. People can use such systems on the web or in an app. Some are free. Some advanced features cost money.

Artificial intelligence has developed over time. It makes everyday life easier and helps doctors, scientists, businesses, and communities. What will AI be like in the future? Only time will tell!

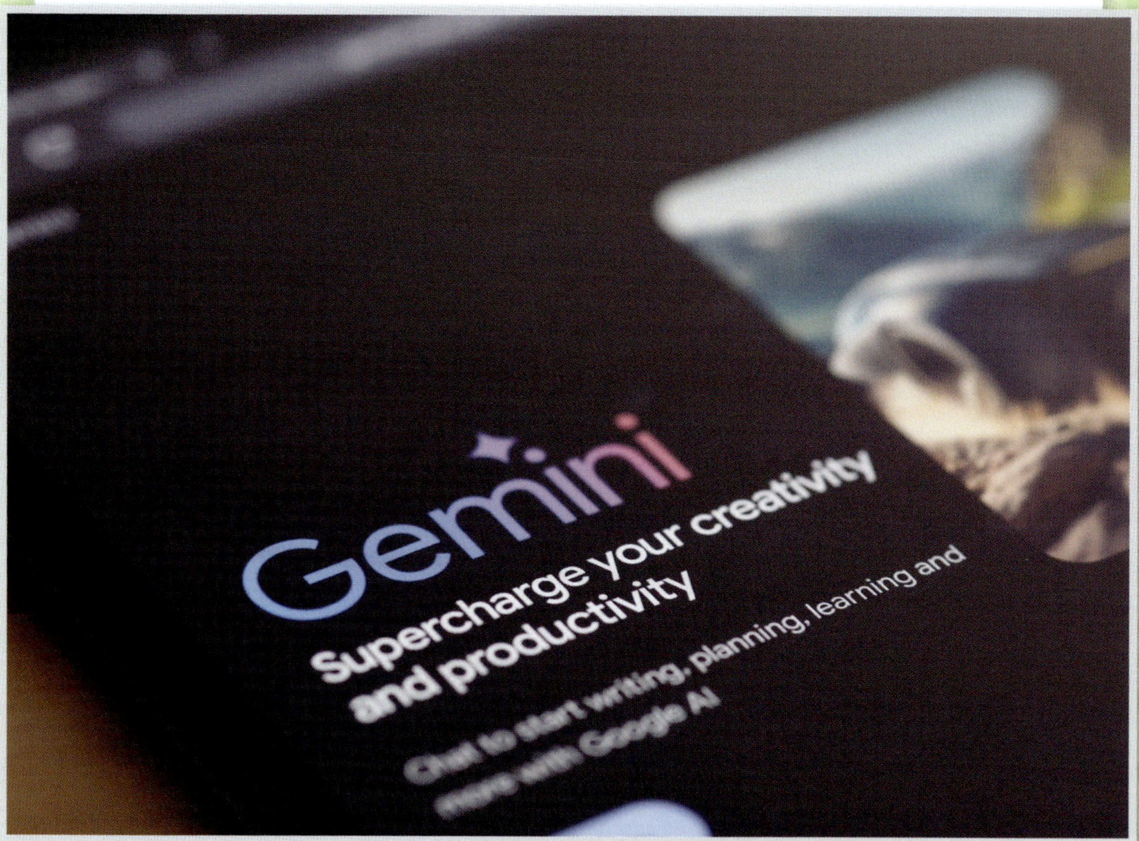


Google released Gemini, then called Google Bard, in March 2023.

# ZARA KHANNA

In 2023 Zara Khanna was a student researcher in computer science. She hopes to invent AI that detects Alzheimer's disease. Khanna works through the She Loves Tech community to empower young girls to explore AI and robotics. When she was only eight years old, Khanna built her first chatbot, Octa. Octa is an online travel bot for families and kids. It helps people find interesting things to do and places to see in cities around the world.

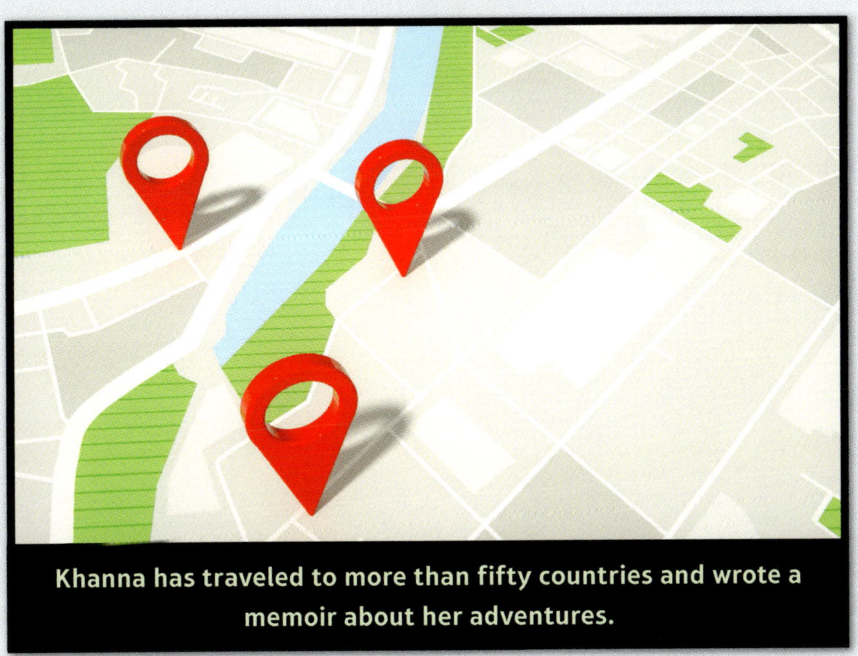

Khanna has traveled to more than fifty countries and wrote a memoir about her adventures.

# Glossary

**algorithm:** a step-by-step way for machines to solve problems

**artificial neural network:** a group of brainlike cells in computers or machines

**chatbot:** any software simulating human conversation with a person

**deep learning:** a form of machine learning

**machine learning:** the way a machine learns without being programmed to do so

**natural language processing:** technology that enables machines to recognize, understand, and use text or speech

**neuron:** a cell in a human brain that allows a person to function

**virtual assistant:** an application that understands voice commands and completes tasks for a user

# Learn More

Britannica Kids: Artificial Intelligence
https://kids.britannica.com/kids/article/artificial-intelligence/390648

Code.org
https://code.org

Harris, Beatrice. *Jobs in Artificial Intelligence*. New York: Cavendish Square, 2024.

Kiddle: Artificial Ingelligence Facts for Kids
https://kids.kiddle.co/Artificial_intelligence

Mattern, Joanne. *All about Artificial Intelligence*. Lake Elmo, MN: Focus Readers, 2023.

*National Geographic Kids*: Your Amazing Brain!
https://www.natgeokids.com/uk/discover/science/general-science/human-brain/

Olson, Elsie. *AI and the Arts*. Minneapolis: Lerner Publications, 2025.

Rathburn, Betsy. *Artificial Intelligence*. Minneapolis: Bellwether, 2021.

# Index



# Photo Acknowledgments

Image credits: Alistair Berg/Getty Images, p. 4; NurPhoto/Getty Images, pp. 5, 27; onuma Inthapong/Getty Images, p. 6; UGO AMEZ/SIPA/Newscom, p. 7; Bettmann/Getty Images, p. 8; Corbis Historical/Getty Images, p. 9; Art Phaneuf/Alamy, p. 10; bankerwin/Getty Images, p. 11; Liubomyr Vorona/Getty Images, p. 12; Jupiterimages/Getty Images, p. 13; Thana Prasongsin/Getty Images, p. 14; Marshall Astor/Wikimedia Commons CC, p. 15; fotograzia/Getty Images, p. 16; The Bold Bureau/Alamy, p. 17; Tada Images/Shutterstock, p. 18; Viaframe/Getty Images, p. 19; Hank Grebe/Getty Images, p. 20; GEOFF ROBINS/Getty Images, p. 21; ShadeDesign/Shutterstock, p. 22; AP Photo/Michael Dwyer, p. 23; FatCamera/Getty Images, p. 24; Marcin Wichary/Wikimedia Commons CC, p. 25; Yana Iskayeva/Getty Images, p. 26; Michael M. Santiago/Getty Images, p. 28; akinbostanci/Getty Images, p. 29. Design elements: filo/Getty Images; JakeOlimb/Getty Images.

Cover: Owen Smith/Getty Images.